FOR JULIEN

Orchard Books, 95 Madison Avenue, New York, NY 10016

Printed in France

10 9 8 7 6 5 4 3 2 1

The text of this book is set in 18 point Trump Mediaeval.
The illustrations are gouache and acrylic paintings.

Library of Congress Cataloging-in-Publication Data
Eduar, Gilles.
[Ailes du crocodile. English]
Jooka saves the day / by Gilles Eduar. — 1st American ed.
p.   cm.
Summary: Jooka thinks he is just an unusual crocodile, until a
pelican teaches him to value the things that make him different.
ISBN 0-531-30036-6
[1. Dragons—Fiction. 2. Crocodiles—Fiction.] I. Title.
PZ7.E2494Jo   1997
[E]—dc21   96-54898

JOOKA
SAVES THE DAY

BY GILLES EDUAR

Orchard Books
NEW YORK

Today, by the banks of the Zimbu River, deep in the Chapichapi rain forest, it's very humid, and much hotter than usual.

In the shade of the trees, the crocodiles are having their siesta. A butterfly flitters lazily by. Even the birds are quiet, dazed by the heat. The only sound is the chuckle of the river flowing along the banks.

BOOM! A great thud awakens everyone. An unusual crocodile wearing a red-striped shirt has bumped into the bridge.

"Whoops! Excuse me. I fell asleep in the water. The current must have carried me here. My name's Jooka-zay-kajoo."

The other crocodiles look at him, grinning. "Have you ever heard such a thing—a crocodile falling asleep in the water? And called Jooka-zay-kajoo?!"

"We'll call you Jooka, okay?" says the biggest crocodile.

"Sure," says Jooka-zay-kajoo. "Jooka—okay—okay. Let's play."

The days go by merrily. More than a month passes. Jooka's new friends like him a lot. He is happy. But unusual. He has antennas and, when he sleeps, wisps of smoke come from his nose. Jooka-zay-kajoo really is a strange crocodile.

One day, while he is fishing with friends, Jooka sneezes very hard—*KACHOO!* Flames shoot from his mouth

and two small, pointy wings pop from beneath his shirt. The frightened crocodiles panic and throw themselves into the river.

What a mess, Jooka thinks. They already know my antennas are weird. Now they've seen the wings on my back. And I sneezed fire!

Jooka sits all alone in the boat for a long, long time. "Why am I different from the other crocodiles?" he wonders, watching a snake slither along.

No one comes back, so Jooka decides to leave. He paddles along in his boat, following the current. At sunset, he comes to a very big river. Lonely, and tired from paddling the whole afternoon, Jooka pulls his boat ashore on a rocky little island. He doesn't notice someone lives there.

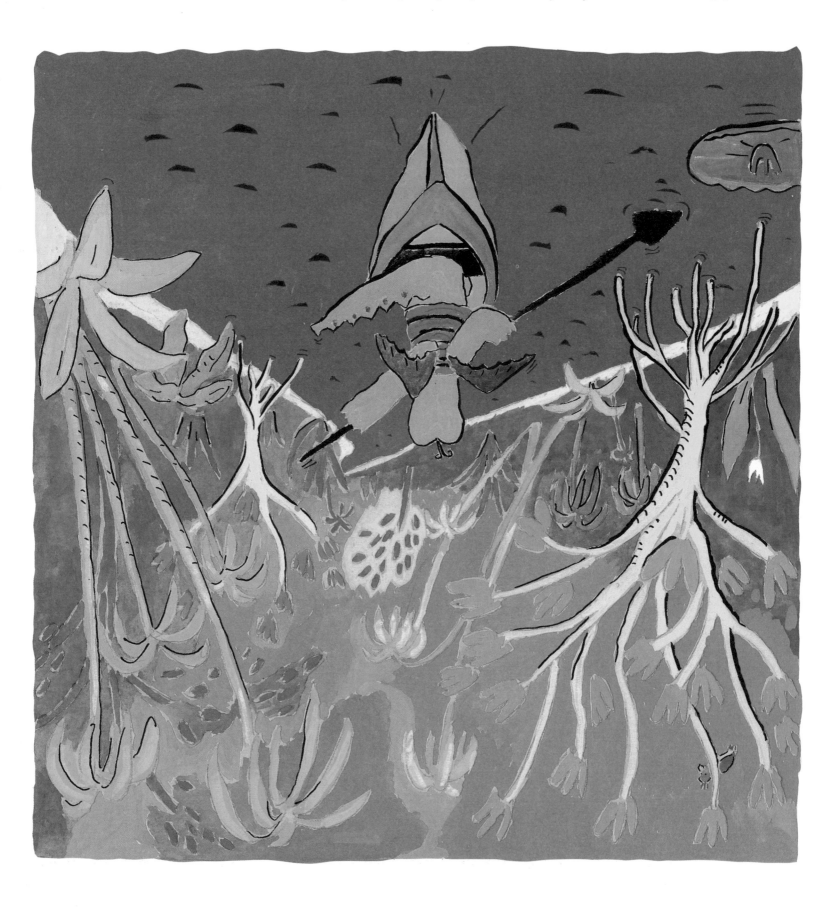

"Good evening," that someone says in a deep voice. Frightened, Jooka whirls around, breathing flames.

"Oh, I'm sorry. I don't know what's happening to me!"

"It's nothing," replies the pelican. "Breathing fire is normal for a dragon like you."

"A dragon?" Jooka asks.

"A dragon," repeats the pelican. "You seem quite surprised."

"I've had lots of surprises lately," says Jooka. "I thought I was a crocodile. A little different, maybe—that's all. My name's Jooka."

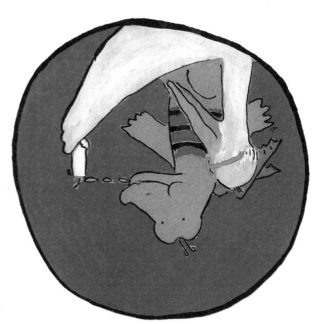

"The differences are gifts. Your gifts, Jooka," says the pelican. "You must learn to use them. My name's Theo." Slowly, under Theo's watchful eye, Jooka practices and practices until he learns to control his flames.

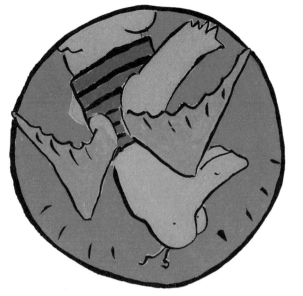

He is no longer ashamed of his wings. Thanks to Theo's training, they've become strong and handsome. The old pelican is proud of his student. Jooka laughs. "No wonder I was an unusual crocodile. I'm a dragon!"

One morning, Theo gives Jooka a big hug. "Good-bye, Jooka. It's time for you to go back. Fly to your crocodile friends and the other animals of the rain forest. They need you."

"Thank you, Theo, for all your help," says Jooka. "I'll visit soon."

The river is magnificent. Shadows of clouds drift across the trees.
In the distance, Jooka sees the crocodiles' bridge.

The bridge hasn't changed. The trees, the river—everything is the same. But where is everyone? It's too quiet.

It's not siesta time, thinks Jooka. Maybe everyone went away. He searches the forest along the river but doesn't find anyone. Then, from high in the trees, Jooka hears a nervous voice. "Jooka! Jooka! Jooka-zay-kajoo!"

Jooka tips his head way back and looks up. Crocodiles are hanging from the branches! A monkey giggles.

"Are you still afraid of me?" cries Jooka.

"No, Jooka," say the crocodiles. "Something terrible happened this morning. We were so afraid that we dashed into the trees, but now we can't get down."

"I'll help you," says Jooka. He carries each crocodile safely to the ground.

"Now, please, what happened?" he asks.

The crocodiles tell him the scary story: "Hunters came this morning. They captured everyone who couldn't escape to the trees—the littlest ones, the oldest ones, everyone who was asleep—and put them in their truck."

Jooka flies quickly up to the top branches of the tallest tree in the rain forest.

Far away, he spies clouds of dust, and the hunters' truck
disappearing into the mountains.

With a few flaps of his mighty wings, Jooka catches up and, lungs full to bursting, breathes his mightiest flames at the two hunters, who fall over each other trying to run away.

Jooka has saved the crocodiles!
"HOORAY! HOORAY FOR JOOKA!"
they cheer.

There is a big twist and shout celebration party along the riverbank, with dancing, loud music, and lots of fish to eat.

All the crocodiles, young and old, big and small, and their dear friend, Jooka the dragon, have great fun.

It's so exciting that no one goes to sleep. Together they watch the sun rise as the new day begins.

"Jooka," the biggest crocodile says, yawning, "you really are most unusual."

"Not for a dragon," replies Jooka, smiling sleepily.